IMAGES OF ENGLAND

CAMBORNE

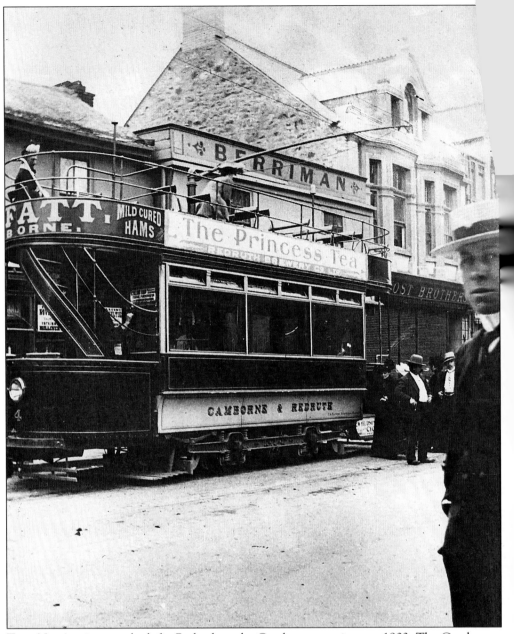

Tram No. 4 waits to embark for Redruth at the Camborne terminus, *c.* 1903. The Camborne-Redruth electric tramway system was opened on 7 November 1902 and closed on 29 September 1927. Two gentlemen, almost Mexican in appearance, stand to the right of the tram while the young man with the boater hat is determined to get into the picture.

IMAGES OF ENGLAND

CAMBORNE

DAVID THOMAS

The
History
Press

An ariel view of the centre of Camborne town. The presence of the tram lines and the Island Site in front of the School of Mines would indicate a date of just before 1927–8.

The cover illustration is a classic view by William John Bennetts of the tram terminus at Commercial Square, Camborne. Tram No.1 is seen shortly after the opening of the Camborne-Redruth tramway system in November 1902.

First published in 1997 by Tempus Publishing

Reprinted in 2010 by
The History Press
The Mill, Brimscombe Port,
Stroud, Gloucestershire, GL5 2QG
www.thehistorypress.co.uk

Reprinted 2011, 2012

British Library Cataloguing in Publication Data.
A catalogue record for this book is available from the British Library.

ISBN 978 0 7524 0765 4

Typesetting and origination by Tempus Publishing.
Printed and bound in England by Marston Book Services Limited, Didcot.

Contents

Samuel John Banbury's grocery shop in Trelowarren Street by J.C. Burrow soon after construction in 1903. The pediment with date and initials has since been removed while the building is now occupied by Superdrug. The window of Barrett's stationery shop is full of postcards for sale. If only one could go back in time!

Introduction and Acknowledgements

This book really has its origins nearly a quarter of a century ago and is the fruit of a gradual process of collecting and gathering photographs, research and information. My maternal grandmother Myrtle Tucker, born in 1899 as well as my two sister paternal great aunts, Lilian and Gladys Thomas (born in 1890 and 1893 respectively), as young Edwardian ladies, were all touched by the postcard collecting craze of that era, and it was their deaths in the 1970s and 1980s which precipitated these collections coming into my possession and which began a process of postcard and photograph collecting of my own area which I have pursued ever since. The collection has now grown to many hundreds of prints, a large number of which are featured here. Indeed the great difficulty has been in not what to include, but what to leave out as the photographic legacy of this area, left by men such as William John Bennetts, John Charles Burrow, E.A. Bragg, E.J. Champion, W.J. Sandry and many others, is truly immense. I have tried as far as possible to select material which has not been published before, conscious of the fact that I am setting down a record of past events for future generations so that nothing might be lost.

There are a great many individuals who have contributed photographs and information in so many ways, over many years, towards the eventual publication of this volume. I would especially like to thank Mr J.A. Osborne, Mr P.R. Bradley, Miss c.M. Blight, Mrs V.E. Berriman, Miss D. Cattran, Mrs T.V. Dunstan, Mr H.C. Blackwell, Mr and Mrs D.G. Bowden, Mrs M.M. Sowell, Mr J.E. Nicholas, the Rector and Churchwardens of Camborne Parish Church, the Camborne Old Cornwall Society Committee, the Redruth Old Cornwall Society Committee, Mr c.J. Parnell, Mr W.P. Glasson, Messrs T.H.E and D. Beckett, Mrs E Reed, Mr J.F. Jotcham, Mr W.J. Watton, Miss L.D. Miller, Mrs Doris Clemens, Mr H.S. Tremelling, Mr and Mrs E A. Ladner, Miss F. Brown, Mrs J. Perry, Mr K.C. Benney, Mrs E.P. Holman, Mrs P.S.J. Hancock, Mr F. Michell, Mrs P.L. Igoe (USA), Mr A.M. Beard, Mr D.A. Elwood, Mr and Mrs W.J. Wills, Mrs H. Jose, Professor A.C. Thomas, Mr J.C.C. Probert, Mr J.A. Williams, the staff of the Camborne Public Library, the Cornish Studies Library at Redruth and the Cornwall Record Office, Truro, as well as Mr R.D. Penhallurick and Miss A.M. Broome of the Royal Institution of Cornwall, Truro. I would also like to pay posthumous tribute to the late Mr and Mrs Frank Hutchin, Mr Alan Curtis, Mrs Doreen Lampshire, Mr William Wood, Mrs E.B. Uren and Mrs c. Bartlett, and also wish to place on record my singular indebtedness to three other people in particular, all now no longer with us, the late Miss G.M. Bray, Mr W.G. Hill and Mr P.G. Southwood. Their powerful reminiscences in the 1970s and 1980s helped to dispel the mists of many intervening decades and provide vivid pictures of vanished Edwardian and later years' events.

I would also like to thank Mr L.J. Bullen for writing the captions to the mining photographs, Mr H.C. Blackwell for access to his notes on Beacon compiled for the centenary of their present chapel in 1995, Mr W.J. Watton of Porthtowan for skilfully copying, enhancing, and in some cases restoring damaged images and Lynn Sheraton for typing out the manuscript. All of this work contributed immensely to the final product.

The photographs on pages 30 (bottom), 40 (bottom), 42, 43 (top), 97 (top) and 125 (top) are included with permission from the photographic archive of the Royal Institution of Cornwall, Truro, while the photograph of the Stray Park shaft at Dolcoath Mine on page 34 (top) is included from the Furze collection with the permission of the Redruth Old Cornwall Society. Information on Edwardian motor cars and vehicle licensing records is included with acknowledgement to Cornwall Record Office, Truro (Reference Number CC3/13/1/1).

This book is not intended to be a history of Camborne town and parish (that volume will one day hopefully be written). Rather it is a personal selection of favourite photographs of my native area, images which record events, stimulate the imagination and hopefully encourage further research and enquiry. The Camborne of today is essentially the product of a thriving nineteenth century mining community in the heart of the chief industrial area of West Cornwall. In selecting material for inclusion I have been guided by section headings which focus on its streets and shops, mining (the town's raison d'etre), the great Dolcoath Mine and Holman Brothers Ltd. in a vital industrial community which was the birthplace of the high pressure steam locomotive. A parish replete with places of worship of every size, type and denomination is also documented, as well as memorable events, formative years at school and a community in moments of leisure. Final chapters focus on the modes of transport of yesteryear, individual personalities and conclude with a selection of material illustrative of a contemporary tour of the parish and district. The approximate timescale of the volume covers the period 1870–1950.

I would wish to offer this photographic tribute of Camborne to the public at large, hoping that it will give them as much pleasure as it did me in compiling it.

I dedicate this book to the memory of my father, Ronald Henry Thomas, (1924–1976), proud to be for 37 years a worker for that great Camborne engineering firm of Holman Brothers, as well as to all those past members of the Camborne Old Cornwall Society who gathered up the fragments which remained, so that nothing might be lost.

David Thomas
Easter 1997.

Vivian's drapery and outfitting shop in Basset Road during enlargement and rebuilding in 1896–7. To the left is R. Taylor's tailors' premises. Staff, workmen and playing children pose for the camera. The rebuilt premises was later fitted out with those wonderful machines for money and change which whizzed around the shop to and from the office. The author's mother worked the shop lift in the late 1930s.

One

Streets and Shops

This picture is the oldest known photograph of Trelowarren Street looking eastwards some time between 1870–1880. The absence of road traffic is very noticeable, with the faint blur of a possible horse-drawn vehicle at the far end of the street in front of the Centenary chapel. Tom Moore's Corner is at the left with a few people standing on the pavement. Trelowarren Street replaced Fore Street as the town's principal thoroughfare in the nineteenth century. It takes its name from Trelowarren at Mawgan in Meneage near Helston, the residence of the Vyvyan family who owned much of the centre of Camborne Town, which was part of their Manor of Illogan, into the early-twentieth century.

Above: Commercial Square, *c*. 1903–4. A horse drinks from the large granite bowl of the fountain, presented to Camborne by John Holman in 1890. The chained water cup for the people's consumption hangs from the left of the upper bowl while the water troughs on the ground were provided for dogs. The waiting tram appears bereft of passengers, but there is quite a crowd outside Henry Berriman's shop window.

Left: Henry Hicks Berriman's cash drapery shop, with a choice array of ladies' hats hanging outside, *c*. 1905. The business was founded in 1860 and the picture shows the new shop premises just after rebuilding in 1904–5, but immediately before the disastrous fire of March 1906.

Commercial Square, with a selection of horse-drawn vehicles, 1906. The granite block on the right side of the fountain's base was used for public announcements on certain occasions. This appears to be a summer scene as the Commercial Hotel boasts a sun blind.

Mr John Brown stands in the doorway of his tailor's shop at No. 83 Trelowarren Street in the 1920s. This shop was originally at No. 39 and stood next down from the corner with North Road. Miss Dunstan's fancy bazaar was the corner shop on its right. The numbered pole was for the Camborne-Redruth Tramway system.

The Camborne Home and Colonial stores at Trelowarren Street, c. 1933. Empire butter as well as Nizam tea at 1s 1d are on display in the window. Leonard Floyd is on the far left. Many will recall Mr R.G. Bruford as the manager of this shop.

The smartly-dressed staff of Horace E. Willis' drapery and millinery shop at No.2 Trelowarren Street in March 1912. Each item in the very full windows has an individual price ticket.

Above: The staff of the Camborne and District Co-operative Society general stores pose for the camera, *c*. 1930. There are many sixpenny items for sale in the windows. This shop then occupied the site of S. J. Banbury's 1903 grocery store. (Compare with the view on page 6.) From left to right: Winnie Webb, Olive Clymo, Marjorie Trim, Kitty Vincent, Anne Warren, Freda Terril, Bert Mitchell, Sylvia Hill, Richard Mitchell (who was lost at sea during the Second World War).

Right: The late Mr Jack Sowell, aged 18, in the doorway of the tobacconist's shop at No. 22 Trelowarren Street in 1938. Gold Block tobacco is advertised at 1s 4d an ounce. John Sowell (1841–1910) was the first of the family to open a grocery shop in the street and was succeeded in business by his son John Garfield Sowell who died in 1934.

Trelowarren Street looking eastwards, *c.* 1905–10. The tramlines are clearly evident. The shops on the left are Henry Berriman (draper), W.H. Smith (bookseller, newsagent and stationer), Edward Rogers (cabinet maker and house furnisher), Horace Willis (draper and milliner) and S.J. Banbury (grocer).

Moncini's shop in Trelowarren Street in the mid 1920s. This premises is now the site of ETS. The shop had a number of functions, selling ice cream (still remembered in Camborne today for its excellent quality), fish and chips, fruit and sweets. Mr Donald Moncini with some of the staff are in the right hand doorway, with his father Antonio in the left entrance.

E.A. Bragg stands at the junction of Trelowarren Street and Union Street to capture this view of 1903. The muddy road is in marked contrast to the tarmac of today. On the left is the Tower House premises of Duckham and Johns, grocer and Italian warehouseman, built in 1887. The turret still forms a focal point in the main street of 1997.

This view was almost certainly taken on the same occasion as that previous, with the eastern half of Trelowarren Street here recorded. The Urban Electric Supply Company Shop is on the left corner, now Norton's fish and chip shop, while on the right is Barnett and Company, cash drapers. Some of the original miners cottages in the street are visible on the right.

Above: Symons's grocery and confectionery shop in Trelowarren Street, *c*. 1900. The doorway of Laity's stocking factory is on the left, while on the right is the window of Tom Bastion's shop.

Left: Berryman's Trelowarren Street premises, *c*. 1930. This shop should not be confused with Henry Berriman the drapers. Its site is now Pooley's butchers shop at No. 103. The shop's hoarding advertises Mr Berryman senior as a wholesale fruit and potato merchant, commission saleman and importer. The upper part of the shop's facade, dating from the late-nineteenth century is an attractive feature.

Gordon Tellam stands in the doorway of M.J. Tellam's fruit and greengrocery shop at No.36 Trelowarren Street, c. 1948–50. This occasion was a Camborne Shopping Week. Today the site is occupied by Iceland.

Mr and Mrs Manhire flank the window of their Trelowarren Street butchers' premises, c. 1910. One wonders what the public health inspectors of the 1990s would have made of all of this! The author recalls seeing rabbits for sale hanging outside a shop in Pendarves Street, Tuckingmill until quite recent times.

A rare shot, by J.C. Burrow, of the junction of College Row, Wellington Road and Church Street, *c.* 1900. The Plough Inn is on the far left and the Miners' Arms on the right. There were once six public houses within a very short walking distance of the parish church. The street corner at the centre, today the site of a health club and garage, has totally changed. Here it is occupied by Mr William John Lee's hairdressers' shop.

Church Street looking east, *c.* 1905–10. The St George's Hall upper extension over the market building was not completed until 1911 subsequent to this view. The original 'Churchtown' would have been merely a row of cottages similar to the Golden Lion public house on the left. Some ladies pause to admire items for sale on a pavement stall outside the parish church railings. The last of these stalls disappeared in 1940.

William J. and Charles Tyack's ironmongery premises opposite the parish church, *c.* 1903. Note the items hanging outside the shop and the contents of the upper windows. Muriel Sara in her reminiscences refers to sitting in one of these windows watching events at the parish church and in the busy street below. The Tyack shop, as Tyack's 1926 Ltd., survived into the 1990s, but is sadly no more.

Miss Belle Oats' boot and shoe shop in Church Street, *c.* 1909. Gas lamps adorn the window which contains individually priced items. Camborne's Edwardian miscreant children were told by exasperated parents, 'If you don't behave, I'll send you up to see Miss Belle Oats'. There she stands in the doorway! The assistant on the left is Sarah Anne Hawke.

Vivian's shop at the north end of Basset Road, c. 1895. The Market House and the front of Tyack's Hotel are in the background. See also the view on page 8. The business, established in 1839, stands at the northern end of the Basset family tenement of Camborne Veor, which extended southwards up Beacon Hill to Trevu House.

Charles Whear's drapery shop next to the 1866 Market House in the Market Place or Commercial Street, c. 1880s. On the left there is also a family grocers and bakery premises, selling flour, oats, meal and bran.

Commercial Street captured by J.C. Burrow,
c. 1900. On the left is c.E. Thomas the
ironmongers, while the shops from the right
inwards are H.T. Williams (outfitter), T.
Heynes (grocer) and W. H. Banfield (tailor).
Older residents refer still to 'Cowboy Heynes'
as he wore spurs in his boots. In the distance a
waggon pauses outside the Public Benefit Boot
Co. shop, which occupied the premises of the
previous Whear's shop at a later period.

Wearne's jewellers and watchmaker's shop
in the Market Place in the 1920s. William
Wearne, born at Pengegon, began business in
a workshop in Centenary Street in 1890 and
subsequently had a shop in Trelowarren Street.
From 1894 he occupied the then newly-built
premises depicted here. After the First World
War a branch shop was opened at Helston.
The Camborne premises also contained a
workshop.

Market Square, *c.* 1900. The landmark premises of the Market House, Town Clock, Assembly Rooms and Camborne Savings Bank (established in 1860) were erected by John Francis Basset of Tehidy in 1866-7. Tyack's Hotel, built in 1795 as the Prince George Inn, is on the right. The Star Tea Grocery Company's shop is on the left, today the Lloyd's bank premises. The photographer has attracted a great deal of interest.

Part of Trelowarren Street's north side, *c.* 1890. The right hand shop is the premises of J.C. Burrow the photographer who also took this view. The cottage on the extreme right is the same site as John Brown's shop, shown on page 11.

22

Cross Street looking westwards in the 1930s. The Masonic Hall was built in 1899 on the site of some cottages. Next door is W.J. Bennett's (photographer) which was adjacent to Toms' the ironmongers. At the far end of the street's skyline is the tall roof of the 1897 Vivian premises in Basset Road.

Fore Street looking south, c. 1910. The houses on the right date from the early part of the nineteenth century. One of those on the left is dated 1889. It was up this hill on Christmas Eve in 1801 that Richard Trevithick drove the world's first steam road locomotive. Hence the 'Camborne Hill' of the famous song.

The 'Island Site' looking westwards in the mid 1920s. All of the buildings to the right of the clock were pulled down in 1928. Stanley's optician's shop is the centre premises, occupied in the 1890s by Tyack the draper and later Kendall's.

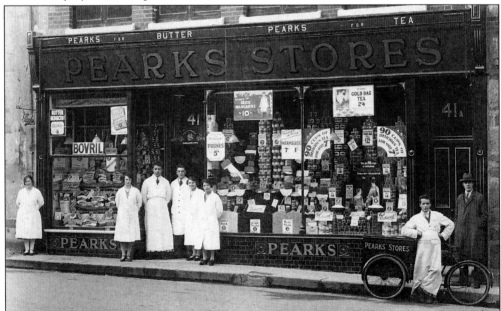

Pearks' Stores at No.41 Commercial Street, *c.* 1920. Prunes are sold for 5d, marmalade at 7d or 1s and Pearks' Gold Bag Tea at 2s 4d. The delivery boy, with bicycle, stands apart from the main group of shop staff.

The 'Island Site' looking eastwards, again in the mid 1920s. All of the buildings to the left of the Midland Bank were demolished in 1928. The fried fish and chip shop was originally occupied by Vivian's Temperance Hotel and Eating House, while the shop with the Lyons Tea sign was a grocery business at what was called Shakerley's Corner in Victorian times.

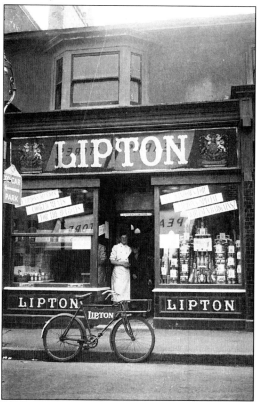

Lipton's stores at No. 38 Commercial Street taken by J.E. Nicholas on Thursday 9 May 1940. In the doorway are assistant William Mitchell and Mrs Emily Snell, wife of the very popular manager William H. Snell who retired in 1946. He was a well-known chess player at the Literary Institute and County Champion of Cornwall and Devon in 1940. The coat of arms which adorned all the Lipton Stores, now called Presto, was by appointment to the late King George V. Prices in the window include Echo margarine 5d (2p), Stork margarine 9d (4p) per 8oz packet, Jacobs Cream Crackers 4d (2p), Cordials 11d (4p), large tins of fruit 8d (4p). Orders from price lists supplied, prepaid, of £2 and upwards were sent to the nearest railway station, carriage paid. The reflection of Pearks' Stores, directly opposite and part of the Allied Suppliers Group is visible. Stores in the group of over 4000 were Lipton, Pearks, Home and Colonial and Maypole. They had three stores in Camborne in 1940.

Market Square looking south towards Basset Road. The Cornish Bank premises of 1893 are on the left incorporating the Capital and Counties Bank. The Market House Inn is in the row of buildings on the right, while Oliver's shoe shop is glimpsed in the far left distance. The delivery boy's basket has the letters SJB on it, standing for S. J. Banbury the grocer (see page 6), implying a date soon after 1903.

Arthur V. Simkin's pawnbroker's shop in Centenary Street, 1906. The proprietor stands in the doorway while his hoarding boasts the business to be of Plymouth and London. To the shop's right is 'Jacky Mitchell's Lane', behind Trelowarren Street. This premises is now a hairdressers salon.

Centenary Square and Wesley Street with the Holman No.1 works on the right, *c.* 1903. The loop system for trams is clearly visible, while the lamp post at the busy junction has long since vanished.

Another view, mainly of the north side of Wesley Street. A tram approaches, while two horses with a flour wagon wait near the Wesley Street Post Office and Mitchell's Economic Supply Stores. This group of shops on the left were later occupied by H.J. Jeffery and son (dairy and confectioner) and the St George Printing Works. The building of the Holman Office block in the distance provides the date of 1911.

Postman Drake poses for E.A. Bragg in the doorway of Tuckingmill Post Office, *c*. 1903. He features in a number of the photographer's postcards and the two obviously knew each other well. A very faint female figure stands behind the postcard display in the window, perhaps the post mistress.

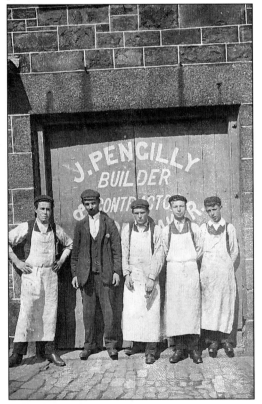

Mr J. Pengilly with his staff of apprentices at No. 47 Pendarves Street, Tuckingmill, *c*. 1905. This was a builder and undertaker's business and at this period it was relatively easy for young lads to obtain a job when leaving school. Unemployment for those over 14 was virtually unknown. KTV Sales now occupy this site.

Two

Mining and Industry

Dolcoath Mine, with the Wheal Harriet compressor house on the left, *c.* 1903. In the background, from left to right are: stamps engine house, the house and stack of the steam driven air compressor, the headgear of Old Sump Shaft (through which may be seen the headgear of New East shaft), the headgear on New Sump Shaft and the 85" pumping engine house.

The Dolcoath Mine. A group believed to have been taken at the collar of the New Sump shaft in the late-nineteenth century.

The Dolcoath Mine at the 440 fathom level, March 1903. On the left is an Under Captain named Rule. Next to him is a member of the Thomas family, while the man leaning on the tram is also a Thomas, a name long associated with the mine.

The Dolcoath Mine, 1893. The 'man engine' at the 234 fathom level which was a means of ascending and descending the mine by stepping on and off the platforms of a reciprocating rod.

Trammers at work near the Williams shaft in Dolcoath Mine at the 490 fathom level, *c.* 1910.

The Dolcoath Mine in the late-nineteenth century. The Californian stamps machinery on the eastern side of the Tuckingmill Valley can be seen.

The Dolcoath Mine in the early-twentieth century. In this photograph the Williams shaft during the course of sinking can be seen.

The Dolcoath Mine in a further close-up view of the Williams shaft when sinking, early in the twentieth century.

The Williams shaft at Dolcoath Mine, in the early-twentieth century. An internal view of the unique Holman-built traversing winding engine.

The Dolcoath Mine in the late-nineteenth century. In this photograph of Straypark shaft the pumping engine house, capstan shears and headgear are visible.

The Dolcoath Mine in the late-nineteenth century. Straypark shaft, the lander and shaftmen can be seen.

A mining scene taken from the east flank of Carn Entral in the late-nineteenth century. It includes Cook's Kitchen, South Tincroft and North Tincroft Mines. Brea village lies in the foreground.

The Tincroft Mine in the late-nineteenth century. A group probably taken at Martin's East shaft. Captain William Teague junior stands on the right in wing collar and bowler hat.

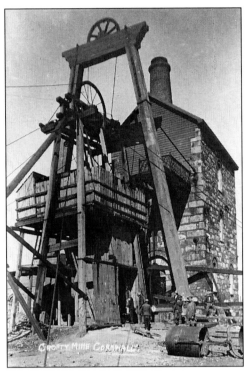

The South Crofty Mine, *c.* 1903. An early view of Robinson's shaft when sinking, with the temporary capstan shears and sinking headgear in place.

The South Crofty Mine, *c.* 1908. Robinson's shaft with all of the plant fully commissioned and showing the horse-drawn tramway. This conveyed ore to the stamps from Robinson's shaft, Bickford's shaft and Palmer's shaft. The latter can be seen on the left.

Robinson's shaft at the South Crofty Mine, *c.* 1903. In the foreground are two boilers on the left and two sets of foundations, one for the Holman horizontal winder and the other for a Fraser and Chalmers steam driven air compressor. Beyond are the 80" pumping engine boiler house and engine house. The wooden permanent headgear and ore bins are under construction and the sheave wheel of the temporary winding engine is part way down the headgear on the right. In the background are Carn Brea and Tincroft Mines.

South Crofty Mine, *c.* 1907. The site of the present New Cooks Kitchen shaft but taken before that shaft commenced. Through the trestle on the left are the calciners and one of the arsenic stacks. The trestle, on which was laid a self-acting double track tramway, is connecting the East shaft to the crusher building under which is an ore bin. From here another tramway leads to the Californian stamps. The rope from the winder ran along the pulley stands to the Eastern shaft.

The Count House and miners at the South Crofty Mine, at the time of the strike in 1939.

TOLVADON TIN STREAMS. TUCKINGMILL.

The Tuckingmill Valley, north of the village of Tuckingmill showing various tin streams and arsenic stacks, c. 1900. In the background are the two Cornish stamp engines at Tolvaddon which was the site of the East Pool Mine dressing floors. On the extreme right are two very tall stacks. One served the arsenic flues of the mine and the other served some of the tin streams arsenic refineries.

The Carn Camborne Mine near Beacon, c. 1900. The concrete water tank had no connection with the mine which closed finally around 1885.

The Great Condurrow Mine, also near Beacon village, 1906. This photograph shows the engine house and headgear being erected at the Neame's (or Woolf's) shaft.

The King Edward Mine (formerly South Condurrow). The Camborne School of Mines took over the property for training of mining students. The scene shows the area around the engine shaft early in the twentieth century.

The King Edward Mine in the early-twentieth century. The erection of the new wooden headgear on the engine shaft can be seen. Note the old pitwork from the shaft.

The Wheal Grenville Mine near Troon, with the old stamps engine and the Western (or Pease's) shaft headgear on the right, c. 1900.

The Wheal Grenville Mine. A group photograph taken outside the Count House early in the twentieth century.

Above: A group of employees outside the Count House at the Wheal Grenville Mine, in the early years of the twentieth century. Not one person is hatless! This photograph was almost certainly taken on the same occasion as the next two pictures.

Left: The Wheal Grenville Mine. Mr Henry Battens and other members of the mine staff outside the Count House, Wednesday 22 February, 1911.

The Wheal Grenville Mine. Mr Henry Battens at his desk in the Count House, 22 February, 1911. He was the mine manager from 1910 to 1913.

The Fortescue's shaft at the Wheal Grenville Mine, 1922. The 90" engine is being dismantled for removal to the South Crofty Mine. The central figure is Mr Abercrombie, Liquidators Manager and on his left Mr Archie Tonkin of John Tonkin & Co., engineers.

The first of three depictions showing the growth of the Holman No. 1 works on the Wesley Street site, today occupied by the Tesco Store. This view depicts the foundry in the 1830s with the miners cottages of Centenary Row East to the rear. Nicholas Holman opened a boiler works at Pool in Illogan in 1801 while his son John opened a further works at Camborne in 1839.

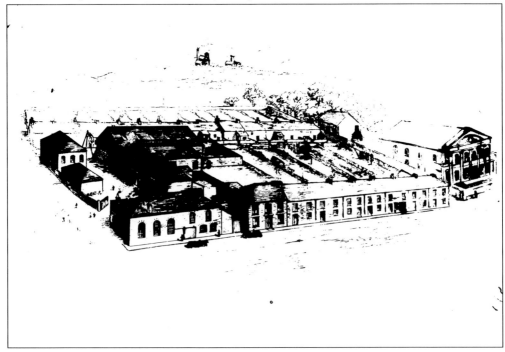

A later view of the No. 1 works in the middle of the nineteenth century. Centenary Wesleyan chapel is on the right, while there is also a row of cottages on the Wesley Street frontage.

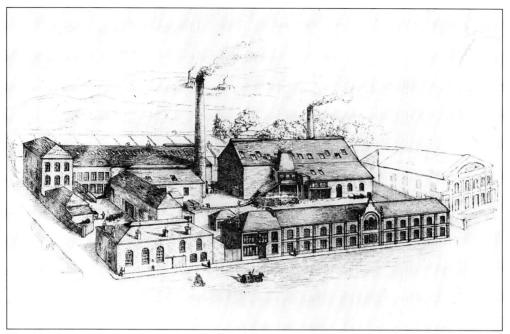

This third view depicts the works, *c.* 1900. The row of cottages in Wesley Street have been replaced by the brick and granite foundry building, while the Centenary chapel has been augmented by the new Sunday school premises of 1887.

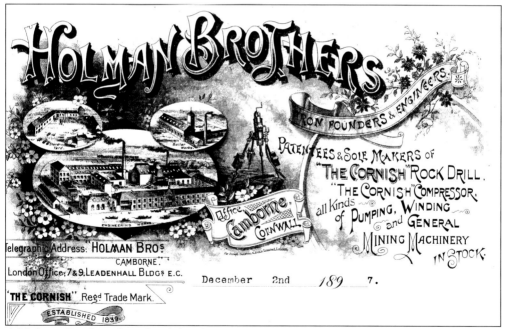

A Holman Brothers' letterhead dated 2 December 1897. It proudly boasts of the type of goods manufactured in large quantities by the end of the nineteenth century, which made the name of Holman synonymous with Camborne and the manufacture of mining machinery and equipment, and renowned world-wide.

A group of Holman employees, *c.* 1887. Mr J.H. Holman stands at the far right wearing a bowler hat. The gentleman on the extreme left with the long black beard is Mr Miller, the Company Secretary.

The Holman office building in Wesley Street taken by J.C. Burrow soon after its construction in 1911. The firm's archives were housed at the top of the tower. Today this is the site of the Tesco store's car park. The author recalls being impressed as a small boy, walking past this building to his grandmother's house in Dolcoath Avenue, at the fine pillars which flanked the doorway. These were hand polished by Italian craftsmen.

Employees at the Holman's No. 3 works, 1905. Back row, left to right: 'Cocky' Vivian, Jimmy Oliver, Jack Udy, Tom Martin, Joe Rodda, Mark Trebilcock, Alfie Bray, Frank Blamey, Jack Tromans, Bert Turner, Bill Daddow, Sid Roberts, Jack Berryman. Second row, left to right: Arthur Thomas, Jack Quick, George Richards, George Bawden, Jack Reed, Billy Gilbert, Ben Cock (Works Manager), F.C. Eddy (Clerk), Edward Arnold, Bill Combellick, Charlie Collins, Bert Tresidder, Howard Willoughby, -?-, Dick Bennetts. Third row, left to right: Bill Eade, -?-, Sam Osborne, Jack Holman, Wilson Uren, Willie Daniel, Willie Curnow, S. Dunn, Charlie Trevena, Bill Clemo, Henry Tonkin, Artie Rosevear, Edwin Bray (Foreman), Jack Vivian, Herbie Brown. Fourth row, left to right: Billy Brown, Johnny Crowle, Freddie Rule, Tom Matthews, Meto Trebilcock, Ernie Capel, Arthur Weekes (Office), Tommy Trevena, Jack Sowden, Sammy Williams, Charlie Vivian, George Chinn, Ernie Trewin.

The employees of Holman Bros., c. 1935. It would be impossible to count the number of men in this photograph, indicative of the strength and importance of the firm at this period.

A Climax works children's party in the mid 1930s. It looks as if a good feed was had by all the participants.

One of the number of sittings in the Holman canteen for the firm's employees in May 1951. This was to commemorate the 150th anniversary of its foundation in 1801.

Three

Church, Chapel
and Salvation

The Parish Church, c. 1870. This is the only known view of the exterior of the parish church before the enlargements of 1878-9 and the building of the second south aisle. The church was restored in 1862 and a new vestry added which is to the right of the central tree. The transept in the centre was known as the Tehidy transept or Basset pew or seat where the squires of Tehidy or their stewards sat. It was added to the church in 1735. This was pulled down in 1878–9, being replaced by a large pew at the west end of the new aisle while the porch and 1862 vestry were moved southwards and built onto the additional aisle on the same site. The east side of the tower has a clock face, the original 'town clock'. This was removed in 1882 when two additional bells were added to complete the peal of eight. The distinctive vane on the tower pinnacle has also since vanished. The high railings to the right of the vestry surround the Rosewarne Harris and Hartley vault.

PARISH CHURCH (ST. MARTIN'S), CAMBORNE

The south front of the church, c. 1930. Compare with the view on the previous page. This photograph shows this prospect of the church as it appeared between the enlargements of 1878–9 and the building of the new church hall in 1963.

1135 CAMBORNE Interior of St Mart

The nave of the parish church looking east in the late 1920s. The flags hanging from the roof were those of the allied nations of the First World War. Most were removed in the Second World War, but four in the chancel survived into the 1950s. The fine brass candelabra were given by the Revd G.B. Hooper in 1911.

50

This fine picture by W.J. Sandry is of the church choir outside the Rectory some time between 1885-90. Canon W.P. Chappel is fifth from the left in the middle row. James Martin, the organist from 1880–1900 is in the back row wearing a spotted bow tie. Also in the back row are John Phillips (third from left) and John Henry Champion (fourth from left). At the far right with beard is William Nicholas Trounson. Leonora Rogers is sixth from the right in the middle row.

Canon William Pester Chappel, Rector (1858–1900), captured in this photograph in the 1890s by Major and Darker of Church Street. He was the son of a Mayor of Truro and a zealous parish priest. He restored and enlarged the church, added two new bells and opened a new Mission room in 1885. In 1898 his health began to fail and he died on 2 February, 1900. Two windows commemorate him in the church.

The church choir in the Rectory gardens, *c.* 1908. Back row, left to right: Tim Haly, W.F. Broad (organist), W. Woodcock, W. Cole, Charles Toghill (crucifer), E. Whitford, S. Smitham, W. Beringer, W.A. Trezize, W. Vivian. Middle row, left to right: George Uren, J. Tucker, W. Trezize, J.H. Richards, -?-, P. Steer. Front Row, left to right: J. Glasson, P. Rogers, P. Phillips, Revd G.B. Hooper, J. Weaver, W. Wood, Jack Hill. The St Martin banner on the left was given to the church in 1904 and the one on the right was an altar frontal of 1736.

A fete showing the men's stall in the Rectory gardens, *c.* 1905. A very fine array of goods is being offered for sale. John Phillips stands on the left.

The interior of All Saints Church, Tuckingmill which was built in 1845. The now vanished oak chancel screen was dedicated on 5 July 1900 with a cross above given by the communicants. As the clergy, but not the oak choir stalls are present this picture must date from 1900–1902. The church's oak reredos was not added until 1913.

The chancel of Holy Trinity Church, Penponds just after the new east window was dedicated in 1909. Between 1896 and 1935 the interior of a very plain building was transformed under the auspices of Canon J.S. Carah. It now contains a very fine series of modern bench ends carved in the traditional Cornish style. The photograph was also taken before the beautiful reredos was added.

The interior of the St John's Roman Catholic Church in Trevu Road, *c.* 1910. In accordance with the taste of the times the altar is festooned with candles. Today the reredos and many of the statues and shrines have been removed in the post-Vatican II era.

The 1840 original Plantation Chapel near Troon, latterly the Sunday school, as seen in November 1964. A typical scene of Cornish village Methodism, which has vanished in many smaller communities through lack of support. Note the oil lamps and the Georgian style pews.

A commemorative group on the steps of Camborne Wesley Chapel on the occasion of the forming of the Wesley Youth Club in 1948. The chapel dates from 1828 replacing an earlier building of 1805 on the site of the present Donald Thomas Day Centre. A Sunday school was founded in 1810.

A group on the steps of the Centenary Chapel on the occasion of the re-opening services after extensive renovations in 1939. Mr C.V. Thomas the Camborne solicitor stands on the left while on the right the man with glasses looking at the camera is Treleaven Charles Quintrell, whose reminiscences of Camborne in Victorian times were exceptional.

Camborne's North Parade United Methodist Free Church Chapel photographed by J.C. Burrow in the 1890s. The interior is typical of a larger nineteenth-century Cornish chapel. The rostrum and fine Gothic organ case are the only visible ornaments.

The interior of the thatched wayside chapel at Roseworthy, c. 1905. The organ, built in 1884, was the first to be made by Mr Fleetwood, the Camborne organ builder of Carnarthen Row. He built his last for the Tuckingmill Primitive chapel in 1923. The Roseworthy organ was sold to Mr J.C. Prisk of Pengegon in the Second World War, but later sold to Osmond's of Taunton. The chapel is said to date from about 1825.

The original Beacon Wesleyan Chapel of 1839, photographed not long before demolition in 1895 to build the new Sunday school. It measured 30 x 22 feet.

The Beacon Wesleyan choir, outside the 1865 chapel premises, *c*. 1908. In the middle row, second from the left is Joseph Henry Williams. In the front row, left to right are: J. Bartle (choirmaster), Mrs Bartle, -?-, Lily Truscott, -?-, -?-, Miss Kennet, -?-, -?-, Mrs Hendra, -?-. What a marvellous array of hats!

The Brea Bible Christian Chapel Band of Hope Tea Treat, 1906. This was held in the field in front of the chapel. The band are present while special stalls or 'standings' have been erected. The level of support is clearly manifest. Today the chapel has only a handful of members.

The Camborne Salvation Army Corps Accordion Band, 1941. Back row, left to right: Denzil Harvey, Winifred Wallace, Gerald Fletcher, Donald Cock, Gladys Holman. Front row, left to right: Lily Phillips, Gladys Thomas, Major Stacy, Rex Roberts, John Pridmore Smith.

Four

Occasions,
Great and Small

The snow thaws in Pendarves Street, Beacon, after the Great Blizzard of March 1891. William John Bennetts points his camera south towards Green Lane and Troon to record this memorable scene. The tremendous depth of the snow can be seen in the centre of the picture

As a result of the Great Blizzard, the Flying Dutchman express train left the rails on the down line between Roskear Junction and the Roskear crossing on 10 March 1891. The engine was named Leopard. In the background the engine house and stacks of the Stray Park section of the Dolcoath Mine can be seen.

A travelling caravan with mobile shop set up for business outside the Pendarves Arms at Beacon. The landlord of the pub was James Henry Bennetts, a brother to William John the photographer. Note also the acrobat performing on the high wire to attract customers. To the right of the pub the stack of Carn Camborne Mine is just visible. The occasion is probably the Camborne Feast celebrations of November 1891.

The scene of carnage at the corner of Cadogan and Mount Pleasant Roads after a terrible motor charabanc accident involving the twenty seater Margie on Saturday 4 October 1924. The vehicle was owned by Messrs W. Reed and Tremayne of Troon and left the village of Troon at 2.15 p.m. A Dorothy May Johns, aged 10, of Chycarne, Troon was killed while 14 other persons were injured. The bus turned over at this sharp bend in the road.

Laying the water mains pipes in Pendarves Street, Beacon, c. 1926. The village's famous landmark stack is visible on the skyline as well as the roof of the Wesleyan Sunday school.

On a very wet Christmas Eve, the procession of steam traction engines forms at the north end of Basset Road, 1901. This was to commemorate the centenary of the first steam road locomotive which appeared in the streets of Camborne on Christmas Eve in 1801, run by Richard Trevithick and Andrew Vivian. The Basset Arms Hotel is on the right while Vivian's huge shop dominates the skyline.

The Trevithick statue dedicated to the great inventor (1771–1833) is unveiled by Prince George outside the library on 17 May 1932. Councillors, inhabitants and school children all watch intently.

Another view of the Trevithick centenary procession as it pauses for the camera in front of Centenary Chapel, 1901. Miners from Dolcoath carry commemorative placards while the councillors stand at the bottom left. In the centre is Harvey & Co's large Aveling and Porter crane engine, while those to the left and right are Burrell 'single-crank compounds'.

A small portion of the procession through the town to mark the centenary of Trevithick's death, at the bottom of Tehidy Road at the junction with Enys Road, 1933.

A vast crowd in Commercial Square gather to celebrate the end of the Boer War in 1902. A speaker addresses the crowd from the front of the Commercial Hotel. All of the buildings, except those at the top right have not survived into the 1990s.

Planting some of the first trees at the Camborne Recreation Ground, c. 1902. The small boy with the shovel is believed to be John Stackhouse Pendarves.

The crowds once more in Commercial Square for the Camborne Carnival in June 1932. The band lead the carnival queen's procession, who sits on her vehicle surrounded by her attendants. Such public occasions as this were always extremely well supported. Alas, it is not so today.

Mr A.E. Dunn the prospective Liberal parliamentary candidate for the Mining Division in the 1910 General Election outside his committee rooms at the Camborne Public Rooms, The Cross. The small boy looking over this magnificent car's bonnet, whose face is half hidden is the late George Bowden (see page 70).

A large crowd assemble outside Henry Berriman's drapery shop in Commercial Square after the fatal fire of 3 March 1906, when two ladies, trapped in the building, were burned to death. The shop was soon rebuilt and the business, founded in 1860, carried on once more.

The new peal of six bells for All Saints Church, Tuckingmill arrives at the Camborne station goods shed in 1931. Mary Howarth stands in attendance. Two further bells to complete the peal of eight were added in 1936. All were cast by Taylors of Loughborough.

The occasion of the Silver Jubilee of the Revd James Sims Carah as vicar of Penponds in 1921. Speeches were held in the vicarage garden. The lady at the table, Miss Mitchell, is not sitting, but standing. She lived in the cottage adjacent to the church gates and sold postcards in aid of parish funds.

The Camborne Salvation Army Corps dressed for the Camborne Carnival, Saturday 25 July 1931. Their costumes help to illustrate the many countries the army worked in. The location is Rectory Road looking east to the rear of the Plough Inn in College Row.

The Troon Tea Treat procession passes south along New Road in 1910. Miss Rule is at the bottom right while the first three men behind her are Mark Trebilcock, Mark Harris and Henry Dennis' son, John Dennis, one of the teachers. The boy to the rear of the line and marked with an arrow with a white braided jacket is the son of Mark Trebilcock. This is postcard no. 5 of a series produced to commemorate the occasion.

Father, mother, child and dog pause in their little vehicle for E.J. Champion against the backdrop of the corner boundary wall of Tuckingmill churchyard as it bends around into Church View Road, sometime between 1905–10. Any indications as to identity would be welcomed.

Five

'Up School'

The Basset Road Board School, c. 1890. This was originally a British school and a site for the building shown was granted by the Basset estate in 1855 out of the tenement of Camborne Veor. This was later taken over and run by the Camborne School Board who replaced it with a much grander structure in the Gothic style in 1893.

Basset Road School mixed infants with their teacher, 1901. The variety of dress is considerable. In the second row from the front and third from the left is the author's paternal grandfather, Charles Henry (Harry) Thomas (1897–1965).

Basset Road mixed infants photographed against one of the school's entrance gates, 1905. Two brothers are in the second row back. These are, on the far right, George Bowden (1899–1981) who became the manager of Williamson's Garage between 1928 and 1964 and third from the right, Joseph Praed Bowden who died in 1980 aged 79.

A further group of Basset Road mixed infants, c. 1907. The boy in the centre row wearing the fancy lace collar must have been teased by the other children!

A girls' class at Basset Road, c. 1907. In the front row and second from the right is Annie Osborne (later Thomas) of Beacon who was born in 1896.

Basset Road, *c.* 1930. In the back row, left to right: Gladys Hendy, Florence Downing and Ivy Osborne while at the front sit Mary Jane Clayton (left) and Miss Carvolth (right).

A class of mixed pupils at Penponds School, 1913. One lad in the front row seems more intent on his feet than the camera and has not had his face recorded. The master on the right is Mr Parnacott.

College Row National School mixed infants, *c*. 1907. This was a Church of England school which commenced in 1844 in the building that is now occupied by AJM Tyres, but moved to new premises further along the street in 1896. The 1896 building is now the site of a block of flats while the St Meriadoc Infants school is based at Rectory Road.

A May Day group in the College Row School playground, *c*. 1912. The May Queen sits in her chair surrounded by her attendants. Such customs were then observed annually.

Another May Day group at College Row School, *c.* 1914. Two of the attendants hold baskets.

A girls' class at College Row, 1915. Front row, left to right: Lelia Jones, Hilda Holman, Florence Roach, Olive Western, -?-, -?-, Adell Butler, May Mitchell, Mavis Rowe, Millie Bray. Second row, left to right: Emmie Warren, Cora Elliott, Bessie Sowden, Gwen Negus, Maud Davies, Ruby Warren, Maud Passmore, Lillie Eslick, Pearl Tonkin, Doris Smith. Third row, left to right: Ethel Maud Bennetts, Elsie Goldsworthy, Audrey Timmins, Violet Davies, Gwen Sanders, Lillie Ivey, Winnie Trezona, Annie Williams. Fourth row, left to right: Lillie Williams, Doris Lavie, Edith Nicholls, Rose Sowell, Meta Hart, Myrtle Govett, Mary Sanders, Olive Angove, Ruth Uren.

A large group of pupils and teachers in front of the Roskear School, in a photograph taken either at an Empire Day celebration or the Coronation in 1911. The schoolmaster on the ladder with the Union Flag is Harry Carveth. The children appear fascinated by the camera.

Roskear Infants School, 1st Class B, *c.* 1917. As in other school groups depicted earlier, the variety of dress is very marked.

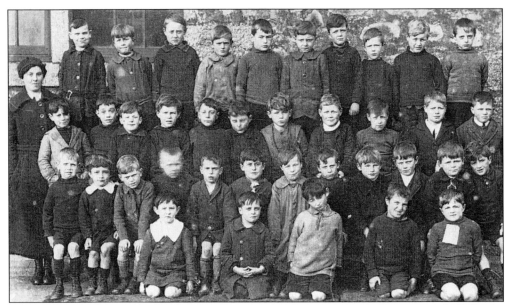

Boys Class No. 1 at Roskear School, 1918. A couple of the subjects have moved while the photograph was being taken. Note also the makeshift class label pinned to the boy at the right side of the front row.

A group photograph of the Roskear boys achieving perfect attendances, 1921.

Roskear boys school, 1943. This class achieved a 100% pass rate in this year for the eleven plus examination. Back row, left to right: Derek Stone, John Corey, Dennis Trinniman, Kenneth Polkinghorne, Tom Whitford, Paul Millett, Peter Kevern, Alan Thomas, Frank Hugo, John Trevenna. Front row, left to right: Shaun Coghlan, Arthur Osborne, Dennis Lampshire, Harry Dawes, Jack Richards (Headmaster), Bobby Bennetts, Brian Trease, Peter Glasson, Eric Wills.

A mixed class at Beacon school, 1922. Miss Pengilly is the teacher standing at the rear right.

Camborne County Girls' Grammar School, Form IVB, 1913.

The Camborne County School cricket team, 1924. Back row, left to right: H. Page, H. Pengelly, M. Jeffree, E. Sara, M. Sara. Front row, left to right: A. Tamblyn, E. Hicks, M. Trewin, A. Bastion, E. Tangye, S. Bray.

Six

Leisure Hours

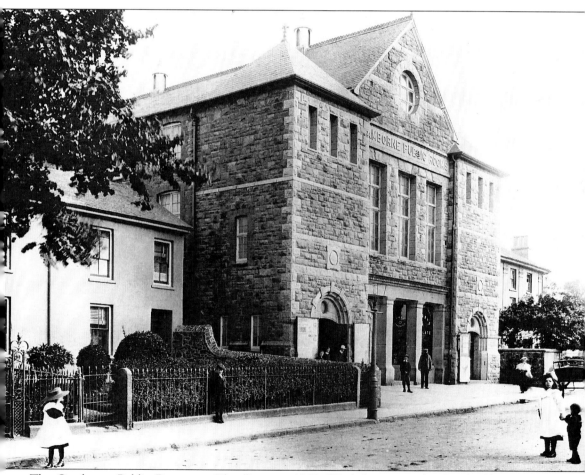

The Camborne Public Rooms, at The Cross, c. 1903. Work began on this fine building in 1889 and it was originally used for public meetings. In later years it became the Holman firm's museum and later still, the Green Baize Snooker Club.

A crowd gathers outside the Public Rooms for the visit of General Booth, the leader of the Salvation Army, 10 August 1904. The evangelist stands near the right hand doorway of the hall. At least three policemen can be seen, as if expecting trouble. Early meetings at the Camborne Salvation Army fortress had witnessed the smashing of windows.

Vincent's Hippodrome opposite Tuckingmill Church in the 1920s. The unusual architecture borders on baroque in its design. After being used as a cinema the building is currently used as a centre for Lazers.

Above: The Camborne Town Band in an unknown location in the 1890s. This remarkably clear picture shows the quality of print that could be produced from a glass plate negative by Victorian photographers.

Left: The Tea Treat day at Troon Square, 1936. This was an important occasion in the religious and social life of the village. The crowd listen attentively as the band perform to the large audience. The occasion is still well-celebrated today.

A photograph of a very early Camborne Rugby Football Club XV, 1884. This was reproduced as a postcard in Edwardian times. There does not seem to have been too strong an emphasis on standard kit at this date. The picture was almost certainly taken at the old Higher Rosewarne ground at Roskear. The stone hedge may be the retaining wall of a mine burrow.

The Camborne RFC team of the 1925–1926 season, photographed in front of the stand at Crane by P.E. Surbey. In this season the team played 42 matches. They won 30 of these, lost 11 and drew 1, running up a total of 595 points for and 247 against.

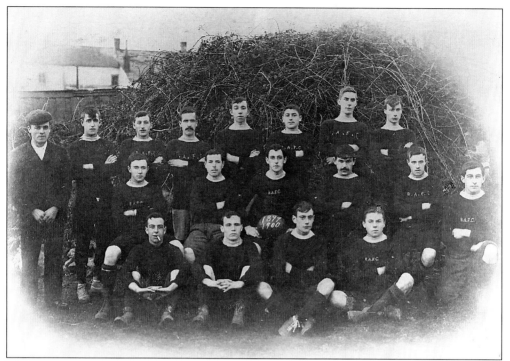

The Beacon Association Football Club team for the 1899–1900 season. One lad in the front row cannot resist the temptation of a cigarette.

Beacon Sports Week in the field near the school, 25/26 June 1936. Standing on the left is Mrs Curnow the champion rolling pin thrower and six inch nail driver in the west! The crowd includes Polly Symons, whom many will remember, Stella Moyle, Boy Stevens, Mrs Andrews, Ron Vivian, Ruth Williams, Zenid Weekes and Dick Dunn.

The Troon Football Club team of the 1908–9 season outside the Grenville Arms in Fore Street, then kept by Matthew Eade.

The Camborne Town AFC team of the 1905–6 season. The photograph was taken in the studio of a little-known Camborne photographer, J. Lukey at No.6 Trelowarren Street. Their striped shirts are very distinctive while the goalie appears to wear a heavy woollen vest.

Camborne's Thursday AFC Team of the 1912–1913 season, at an unknown location.

The Holman Works Choir of 1924. Mr Guy Hill recorded the names for posterity. Back row, left to right: P. George, A. Jenkin, H. Trezona, J. Thomas, Revd W.A. Bryant, W.G. Hill, N. Tromans, K. Williams, T. Williams, W. Harvey. Centre row, left to right: R. Williams, R. Dunn, F. Godolphin, R.H. Davies, A. Rule, S. Dudley, K. Hancock, W. Bersey, E. Pearce, A. Jones. Front row, left to right: W. Dudley, F. Waters, W. James, H. Pascoe, A.S. Tredrea, J. Tromans, W. Hancock, J. Rule, J. Thomas.

THE RECREATION GROUNDS, CAMBORNE.

The Recreation Ground, *c.* 1910. At this time there was no division between the ground and the football field beyond, the site of which was donated by A.F. Basset of Tehidy in 1897.

A tennis group at Miss Vivian's courts at Pengegon House in the late 1920s. Miss Vivian sits in the middle of the centre row. Florrie Major is the girl in the same row on the far left. Miss Vivian was a keen supporter of the North Parade chapel.

Coronation Day, 1911. A crowd has gathered at The Cross to watch the procession of school children. The Troon Council school follow behind their banner waving Union flags, walking down from the railway station. The library is situated behind the photographer.

The same occasion as the previous picture. The procession has reached the football field and before the end of the proceedings coronation mugs and medals would have been distributed as keepsakes.

Playtime outside the post office at Pendarves Street, Tuckingmill, c. 1903. A message on the back of the postcard states that the young child in the doorway was put outside to have its picture taken but the photographer also captured the lady in the black dress.

The tableaux entitled The Brahmin Wedding which was presented at the Missionary Exhibition held at the Camborne Public Rooms from 10–18 June 1909. The whole event was called 'Cornwall beyond the seas' and the bride was called Dorothy although her surname is unknown.

Seven

Transport

One of the earliest motor cars to appear on the streets of Camborne, c. 1903. This splendid vehicle, registration no. AF 31, was a 5 horsepower Panhard with a blue and white tonneau body and red wheels. It was registered to William Rich of Trevu on 28 December 1903 for private use and weighed 13 cwt. The registration was cancelled on 11 October 1904.

Squire Pendarves of Pendarves sits in the back seat of this Austin, accompanied by other members of his family. He died in 1929 and this picture was probably taken not long before his death.

J. Carah Roberts' butcher's van, registration AF 7391, pauses outside his shop in the east facade of the Market House. Ernest Trathen's fruit shop is to the right of the vehicle. The reflection of a portion of the Island Site premises can be seen in the shop's window, suggesting a date in the mid 1920s.

In 1933 there was a trades exhibition held at the Camborne Skating Rink in the Market House, organised by the Chamber of Commerce. This car, a Morris Ten saloon deluxe was the exhibit sent by Williamson's Garage of Church Street. Note the traffic lights which gave the familiar green, amber and red signals. These were discontinued at the end of the year as it was thought to lead to confusion. Edwin Mann (Sonny) stands in the background.

The interior of the vehicle shed at Williamson's Garage, c. 1936. The pick-up truck in the foreground was adapted from the body of a Rolls Royce Silver Shadow.

The tram terminus at Commercial Square by J.C. Burrow, *c.* 1902. Single deck tram No. 5 waits to embark for Redruth. The long straight of Trelowarren Street runs away behind the tram, with a glimpse of Centenary chapel in the distance.

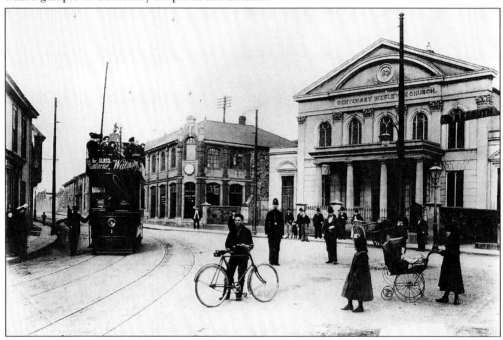

Centenary Square, again photographed by Burrow, *c.* 1903. Tram No.1 is advertising Walmsley's glass shop, while the Holman works, now the site of Tesco's lie beyond. The Centenary Wesleyan chapel was built in 1839 as an overflow chapel to Camborne Wesley, because of a revival at that time.

Tram No. 4 in Trelowarren Street, *c*. 1904. Its young conductor is L. Dudley. Shops to the right include the Cornwall Laundry Co. and Lobb the draper. The trackway divided at this point and the terminus is situated behind the photographer.

Tram No.1 heads down Pendarves Street at Tuckingmill, *c*. 1905. Horse-drawn vehicles carefully avoid the tram lines. Many more shops are evident in comparison to the 1990s. On the extreme right is Benallack's premises, a carpenter and undertaker.

Camborne Railway Station Crossing on 28 February 1896. Note the small wooden crossing keeper's hut and the old station building dating from earlier in the nineteenth century. The new station building is under construction at the far left.

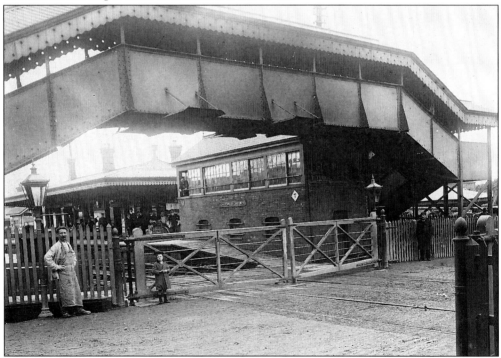

A similar view to the previous photograph, c. 1905. This is the station that many of the town's older residents will remember. The canopy over the bridge was removed in 1940 while the author recalls when the signal box was made redundant at 11.11 a.m. on Sunday 7 June 1970.

E.A. Bragg must have pulled a few strings with the railway authorities to be allowed to take this view of the station from the track, *c.* 1903. Normally the level crossing gates were only closed across the road when a train was approaching.

A '49XX' class engine pulls into the station's up platform in 1953. The goods shed and yard were still very much in use at this time, but were abandoned in the mid 1960s and are now the premises of Magnet Joinery Ltd.

J.C. Burrow has taken the opportunity to capture this view for posterity, with the staff of the Camborne Posting Company sprucing up their many horse-drawn vehicles outside the Commercial Hotel, *c.* 1903. The hotel was used by commercial travellers but after the Second World War became the Studio Theatre. It was demolished in the mid 1950s.

William Quintrell poses for E.A. Bragg with his fruit and vegetable cart, outside the cottages at Illogan Churchtown, *c.* 1903. William was also an amateur poet and published his Original Cornish Poems in 1911.

The famous Trewinnard coach, dating from around 1700 but now housed in Truro Museum, pauses outside the Commercial Hotel, as it is conveyed by Tower House in Trelowarren Street on a Duckham and Johns' delivery wagon. The driver, Mr Tyler, stands on the left and his boss, Mr Borlase, wearing the bowler hat, stands behind him. It travelled up on a Friday in March in 1909 from St Erth to Truro and was stored temporarily at the County Carriage Works at Lemon Quay. By late 1910 it had been restored at Bristol by J. Fuller & Co. It returned to Truro in September 1917 and was insured for £250.

Tregenza's 'Up to Date Chip Potato Car' at Dolcoath Avenue, c. 1920s. Thankfully the chip fat never ignited the wooden vehicle, much to the relief of the occupant and horse! As this is Car No. 3 there must have been at least two other similar vehicles.

Younger Camborne residents will not recall this bus station by the fountain in Commercial Square photographed in the late 1930s. Here four of the No. 33 buses to Redruth are drawn up for the camera. One wonders what the occasion was.

A 26 seater National bus on the Penzance-Hayle-Redruth-Truro run waits in Church Street, c. 1930. To the left are the Miners' Arms public house, Eva's butcher's shop and the Williamson's Garage. Note also the petrol pump further along the street outside Tyack's ironmongers shop.

Eight

People, Personalities and Characters

This group stand inside the east gate of Camborne Churchyard, *c*. 1906. At the bottom left, with linked hands are the five children of Edward Hill, the Rectory gardener who came to work for Canon W.P. Chappel from Gorran in 1890. The late Guy Hill is the small boy at the bottom left, born at Rectory Cottage in 1902. From 1939 he lived at 2B Manor Road and effectively lived all his life in the same road. His small brother Jack is dressed as a girl, a common custom at this period. To the rear left is Charles Bennetts, the Church Sexton who died in 1926 and far right Mr Behenna, the printer from Fore Street.

The Revd George Brereton Hooper, Rector 1900–1934, stands in the Rectory garden rockery created by Edward Hill in 1903. A lot of his ministry took place in Cornish mining parishes as from 1893 to 1900, he was the vicar of St Just in Penwith. Known as 'Parson Hooper' he delighted in his Rectory gardens, did much to help the poor and beautify the parish church, although at times was considered a little eccentric. He is still remembered locally.

The Revd Douglas Edward Morton who succeeded Parson Hooper in 1934. He graduated from the London College of Divinity in 1895 and remained Rector until 1944 when he resigned the Living, being in turn succeeded by the Revd George Frederick Sandfield in February 1945. Mr Morton is remembered as the perfect gentleman.

The Parish Church Cricket team photographed in front of the Rectory, c. 1899. Back row, left to right: Miss M. Chappel (the Rector's daughter), ? Cadwell, E. Williams, J. Kemp, H. Clymo, W. Southgate. Centre row, left to right: E. Ivey, E. Uren (Captain), A. Gill, c. Phillips. Front row, left to right: H(?) Williams, R. Williamson, S. Keast.

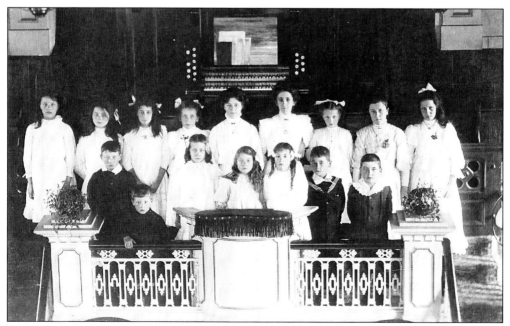

A Band of Hope group captured on the rostrum at Brea Chapel, c. 1905. The company went around to different chapels giving entertainments. The girl on the extreme right is Florrie Brown.

A group outside the Beacon Sunday School building, on the occasion of a mission or revivalist meeting, *c.* 1921.

James Bennetts of Beacon, *c.* 1864. In 1861 he was both grocer and mine agent. A relatively young man of 39, he died of fever in Havana, Cuba on 18 July 1865. He was the father of William John Bennetts (1850–1943) the Beacon, Camborne and Hayle photographer who recorded so much for posterity with his camera.

Five of the nine sons of Captain Josiah Thomas (1833–1901) of Dolcoath Mine, taken at Tregenna, Camborne, *c.* 1895. Back row, left to right: Joseph Vivian Thomas (1870–1927) a solicitor at Penzance and its mayor in 1902, Albert Ernest Thomas (1872–1927) an overseas mining engineer. Front row, left to right: Frederick William Thomas (1863–1933), accountant and company secretary of the Dolcoath Mine Ltd, Josiah Telfer Thomas (1864–1935) a Camborne doctor, Charles Vivian Thomas (1859–1941) the Camborne solicitor, county councillor and alderman.

Captain William Cock Vivian in old age. He attained the distinction of becoming a centenarian in 1919, but died later the same year. The Vivian family were very extensive in Camborne with residences at Reskadinnick and Camborne Veor. W.C. Vivian was one of the nine children of Captain Joseph and Nanny Vivian. A brother, Joseph, of St Maradox Villa in Tehidy Road lived to be 95 years old.

John Charles Burrow in Masonic regalia, c. 1910. The Burrows were a Truro family before coming to Camborne and were involved with the Free Methodist chapel there. Once in Camborne they joined the North Parade United Methodist Free church. In 1893 Burrow, with his assistant Herbert Hughes, perfected the science of underground photography with magnesium flares in the Camborne mines. He had a photographic business at No.38 Trelowarren Street and died in 1914.

A postcard produced to solicit votes for Mr A. Edward Dunn in the 1906 General Election. Camborne was then in the Mining Division Constituency rather than Falmouth and Camborne as it is today. The result of the 1906 poll was Dunn (Liberal) 4,614; Hewitt (Conservative) 2,384; Jones (Socialist) 109. The Liberal majority was 2,230.

Mr. A. EDWARD DUNN,
Liberal Candidate for the Mining Division.

The Camborne Urban District Council of 1932–3, outside the Council Offices at The Cross. Back row, left to right: J. Northey, H. Stephens, J. Bastion, H.S. Bond, W.A. Maclean, W. Frayn, *c.* Eddy, B. Kelly, W. Uglow, S. Haslett, H. Taphouse, L.T. Fiddick, R. Eddy. Front row, left to right: J.J. Bailey, J.C. Roberts, J. Trerise, W.A. Luke, J.F. Odgers, D.W. Thomas, Dr. J. Telfer Thomas, J.E. Turner, J. Williams.

William Quintrell the Camborne poet, photographed in W.J. Bennetts' studio, *c.* 1902. On the slate is a copy of his poem entitled 'Camborne Feast' referring to Mary Ann's opinion of the new street cars or trams to Redruth which came into use on 7 November 1902.

James Thomas (1848–1934) photographed by E.J. Champion in the former's garden at William Street, c. 1910. Mr Thomas was a great antiquarian and collector and is here depicted with some of his treasures. He was employed as a postman, but his chief claim to fame was becoming the first Cornish bard for 1,000 years at the St Buryan Gorsedd in 1928. He had earlier been inducted into the Welsh Gorsedd at Treorchy in 1899. Mr Thomas had his own name engraved on his tombstone some years before his death, much to his neighbour's consternation.

The little girl shown is the late Miss Gertrude Millicent (Millie) Bray (1904–1994) with her grandfather Robert Henry Roskelly in 1910. We know quite a lot about this occasion as there is a verse on the back of the postcard composed by R.H. Roskelly.
'Granfer and Millie the rent went to pay, visiting Mr Champion on the way; in they went hand in hand, out they came looking so grand; now to Naraguta they're gone to stay, from over the waters far away'.
They would have walked from Miss Bray's birthplace at No.33 William Street to No.2 Carnarthen Street for this photo to be taken. Subsequently the card was received at Naraguta on 25 November 1910. Miss Bray, as a church worker held offices under every Rector of Camborne in the twentieth century to date.

Mr William Wood stands outside the door of the cooperage or barrel makers shop which faced up Gurney's Lane in the early 1900s. The site was at the back of what until very recently were the SWEB showrooms in Commercial Square.

A group of railway gangers or trackmen pause from work outside the front of Roskear Junction signal box, c. 1905. The box, like that at the station dated from the mid 1890s. There was also another signal box east of this one at Dolcoath Siding.

A character often seen in Edwardian Camborne was 'Organ Joe' here depicted by E.A. Bragg of Illogan, c. 1903. He roamed the streets with his portable barrel organ as a means of support. It is said that when he died hundreds of pounds were found sewn up in the lining of his coat.

This unknown lady was taken by E.J. Champion, sometime between 1905–10. Perhaps this is her Sunday best. Just look at her magnificent black cape and bonnet. There is a lot of character in her face. One would like to know a little more about her.

Nine

Around and About
the Camborne District

South Terrace looking westwards, c. 1906. The passers-by seem torn between getting their faces recorded by the camera or admiring the new fangled motor car. The author's great aunt, Lilian Thomas, born in 1890, peeps over the garden wall of Basset Cottage at the far left.

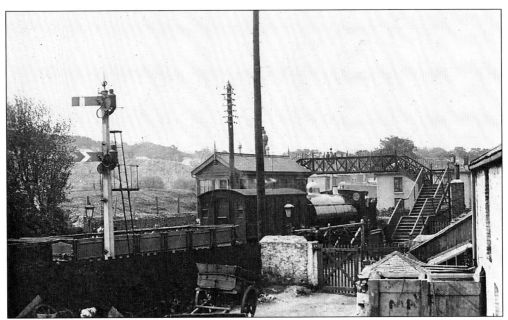

The scene over the photographer's wall at the back of No.2 Carnarthen Street as E.J. Champion records Roskear Junction, c. 1905. A train is entering the North Roskear branch line which led to the boiler works. The signal box, which opened in 1895, is still in use today. To the rear left the burrows of Camborne Vean mine are visible.

The west end of Dolcoath Road, c. 1903. At this point the North Roskear branch line crossed both Dolcoath Road and the main road between Camborne and Redruth. At the bottom left are the lines of the Camborne-Redruth tramway system. This is now the site of Tesco's roundabout.

Roskear Row looking westwards, *c.* 1912. This is a typical Camborne street of miners cottages constructed by the hundreds in the nineteenth century. The level crossing gates belong to the same North Roskear branch as in the previous two photographs. E. Penrose advertises paints, oils, varnishes and wallpaper for sale.

The First World War British tank which stood close to the entrance of the Camborne Recreation Ground, between the wars. Generations of children played on it, but it was removed for scrap during the Second World War, in a very poor condition. The tank bears the numbers 4085 and 83.

The now vanished and world famous Camborne School of Mines building, which served generations of students seeking to learn the practical and theoretical details of mining. Some students talk to their colleagues from an upper window in this mid 1930s view. The building was constructed in 1882 but was demolished to make way for the first Camborne Tesco store.

Leaving the town in a westerly direction, *c.* 1950. This is the scene at Glasson's Garage with its Shell and BP pumps. The garage was opened by Mr Howard Glasson in 1934. In recent years the bungalow has given way to the forecourt of a much larger Shell garage on the busy exit road to Treswithian.

The bottom of East Hill, Tuckingmill looking westwards to Camborne, c. 1903. A crowd has gathered outside the Tuckingmill Hotel while at least three of the children are playing with hoops. A wagon enters the main gate of Bickford Smith & Co's Safety Fuse works. This life-saving device for blasting was invented by William Bickford in 1831, inspired by observing the Illogan miner Thomas Davey spinning rope in his rope-walk.

The 1843 Tuckingmill Wesleyan Chapel, c. 1903. One of three Methodist places of worship at one time in the village and here photographed by E.A. Bragg of Illogan. The chapel, meeting latterly in the 1927 Sunday school premises, finally closed in 1996. Both the other chapels are now also closed.

Pendarves Street, Tuckingmill, probably taken on the same occasion as the previous photograph. The children seem oblivious to the electric tram which is en-route to Redruth.

A scene at Knavegoby, c. 1910. The photographer has captured the final days of the ruined house on the right, occupied in the nineteenth century by the Thomas family. Captain Charles Thomas of the Dolcoath Mine who died in 1868 lived here, while the house would have witnessed the formative years of Captain Josiah Thomas, born in 1833. Another house was later built on the site.

Beacon Square, c. 1905. A large crowd has gathered, determined to get into the picture. Two shops, now long since vanished, are visible in the row of houses of Pendarves Street. The Wesleyan Sunday school building was constructed in 1895 on the site of the original 1839 Beacon chapel. The gable cross, when erected, scandalised some local Methodists who considered it popish! The Beacon Post Office lies away to the right, kept by the family of William John Bennetts the photographer.

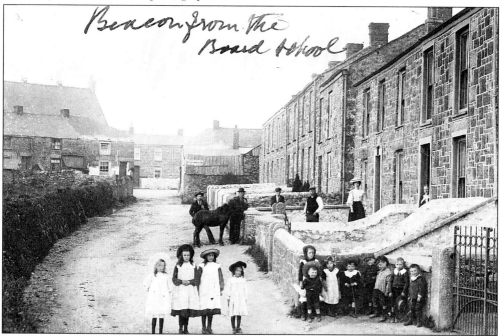

A view looking from the Beacon School in Tolcarne Road back towards Pendarves Street, c. 1905 . The roof of the 1895 Sunday school is at top left, while the terrace of houses on the right were built in the 1870s.

Beacon Square, *c.* 1935. Mr Ben Thomas stands outside his shop with his wife Ada and staff Betty Nicholls, Ida Penrose, as well as Robert Burley the delivery boy.

John Bartle's shop at Beacon when it was owned by May and Lillie Ford, *c.* 1935. Outside stand Cyril Ford and Miss Penrose. The doorway on the right was the entrance to Leslie Moyle's barber's shop.

The interior of the 1865 Wesleyan Chapel at Beacon decorated for a harvest festival in the 1930s. This was an unusual building with apse and transepts, but sadly not a trace of it remains today. The congregation meets in the 1895 Sunday school building. Note the elegant classical organ case.

This chapel was the Higher Condurrow Primitive Methodist Church, built in 1888 but now demolished, c. 1940. Condurrow also had a small Wesleyan chapel, but this too has ceased to be used for worship.

Troon Square, c. 1900. Crowds gather to watch the departure of a number of horse buses or jersey cars possibly for a chapel outing. The shop to the rear left was kept by a Mr Trebilcock, but today trades under the name of Troon's Spar shop. The buses were run by Mr William Henry Berryman, who was also a coal dealer.

Fore Street, Troon, looking north, c. 1905. The lads with horse and cart seem a little too young to be left in charge of their vehicle, while another boy kneels thoughtfully in the road to the left. On the skyline are the roofs of the 1863 Troon Wesleyan chapel and Sunday school.

118

The 1840 Plantation Wesleyan Chapel building in November 1964. Its interior is shown on page 54. This was the original chapel premises but was later used as a Sunday school, replaced by a new chapel on the other side of the road, which is now closed and converted into a house.

The Square at the centre of E.W.W. Pendarves's 1845 'model' Gothic village of Treslothan, c. 1905. The vicarage stands on the right, while the cross within the railings was originally a Pendarves memorial, later converted to a war memorial after the First World War.

The road at Higher Penponds, c. 1930. This was the oldest part of Penponds village with a settlement probably dating from the Middle Ages. The church hall stands on the right, built in the 1870s as a Mission Room as the Bishop of Exeter would not allow Miss Butlin, the vicar's daughter, to lead services in the Penponds parish church.

The village square at Penponds with the post office on the right, c. 1930. The original Hayle Railway, which opened in 1837 from Hayle to Redruth, once passed very close to this spot.

Church Road looking south near the church gates, Penponds, *c*. 1930. The bakery is in the centre of the photograph while just to the right of the railway arch stands the 1844 Bible Christian chapel.

A peaceful scene at Penponds Mill, *c*. 1930. There are many fine walks to be had in this area. Nearby stands a stone clapper bridge of great antiquity.

H. Darlow Wootton of Redruth photographs the library at Penponds Vicarage, c. 1910. This house was built for the Revd James Sims Carah in 1906. The vicar was a great collector and antiquarian and this is reflected in the decor of the house.

The dining room at Penponds Vicarage. The house also possessed a private chapel.

Looking from the village of Barripper back towards Camborne, *c.* 1900. W. Eva's blacksmith's shop is on the right. Three thatched cottages are in evidence while around the corner to the left is Adjawella chapel.

A further view of Barripper looking east, *c.* 1910. William Luke's grocery shop is on the left. The name 'Barripper' is derived from 'good lodging' and the village contains the St Michael's Mount Inn, thought to be a pilgrim's hostelry in mediaeval times.

The village of Kehelland looking north to the fields near the cliffs, *c.* 1910. The Wesleyan chapel building on the left dates from 1891 and replaced an older chapel of 1830 which became the Sunday school premises.

Ancient thatched cottages at Roseworthy on the old road between Camborne and Hayle, *c.* 1930. Regrettably these have vanished. The village lies half in Camborne and half in Gwinear parishes, while the manor of Roseworthy was, before about 1800, the property of the Arundell family, like Connerton, its near neighbour.

Pendarves House, another vanished piece of Camborne's architectural heritage, here captured by Gibson's view, *c*. 1900. Nearby there was an ornamental lake while the grounds once possessed a fine grotto of mineral specimens. The Pendarves family prior to the death of William Cole Pendarves in 1929 were important local land and mine owners. The house was demolished in the mid 1950s.

The annual Tea Treat of the Illogan schools, by the lake at Tehidy Park on 15 July 1904. The occasion seems much enjoyed by children and teachers alike. The great mansion was rebuilt and enlarged in the 1730s and 1860s, but fell victim to a fire on 26 February 1919. The figure at the great central window is believed to be Mrs Basset.

Gwithian Churchtown, *c.* 1903. The church was heavily restored by the Victorians and the ground plan totally altered to a smaller building. The lych gate is made up with an arcade arch from the mediaeval church, while the tower still contains three bells of 1753.

The village of Gwithian, sometime between 1910–15. The church tower is just visible above the trees while in the foreground stands the thatched Wesleyan chapel. The Revd John Wesley and others were granted a lease of a piece of ground for a chapel building in 1771. In the sand dunes near the village lies the buried oratory of St Gothian.

The sands at Portreath beach, probably on a Bank Holiday Monday, c. 1903. On these occasions one dressed up to go on the beach, unlike the 1990s! The area at the back of the sands was known as the Green which does duty today as the car park.

Visitors pause to marvel at the excavations of the Roman Villa at Magor Farm in 1931. This was the result of a chance discovery. The remains were later covered over to preserve them and are no longer visible. There was intense speculation as to the exact date of these buildings.

FISHERMAN'S COVE, NORTH CLIFFS, NR. CAMBORNE.

A strong tide at Fisherman's Cove, North Cliffs, *c.* 1910. These shores have seen many wrecks and there have been incidences where the shipwrecked have vouched for the ferocity of the men of Camborne who plundered the stricken vessels. Galena or lead-silver ore was also mined in these cliffs in the nineteenth century.

43236. GODREVY LIGHT, NEAR ST. IVES.

The close of day. Sunset at Godrevy Island, Gwithian, *c.* 1920. A scene familiar to many Cambornians and a fitting place to end this pictorial story of the Camborne area.